With its small-sized format or availabil[ity]  an iPod app, *New Daylight* is a great w[ay of] finding your way into the Bible day by d[ay. It] contains all the Bible readings as well a[s] helpful notes on them by many differen[t au]thors, so you don't need to carry a Bible with you.

You'll find more about how to get into *New Daylight* on pages 21–23. But first, enjoy the messiness of God, the messy lives of his people through the centuries and the messy plans he has for your life as the marvellous messy story unfolds in the 14 short chapters of this sample pack.

If you're reading it with your children, or if you think best when you're doodling, you might like to draw in the margins and make it even messier...

Lucy Moore

MESSY CHURCH TEAM LEADER

Visit the Messy Church website **www.messychurch.org.uk**

Genesis 1:1–2; Acts 2:1–4 (NIV)

Messy birthday

In the beginning God created the heavens and the earth. Now the earth was formless and empty, darkness was over the surface of the deep, and the Spirit of God was hovering over the waters... When the day of Pentecost came, they were all together in one place. Suddenly a sound like the blowing of a violent wind came from heaven and filled the whole house where they were sitting. They saw what seemed to be tongues of fire that separated and came to rest on each of them. All of them were filled with the Holy Spirit and began to speak in other tongues as the Spirit enabled them.

We never start from nowhere: God has always gone before us and goes ahead of us. In our first passage, we see the planet right back at the beginning as it lay huddled in darkness, like a baby in the womb before it bursts into light and life. Even before that beginning, though, before there was any shape or pattern to anything on earth, the Holy Spirit was brooding over everything, poised for action, ready to turn the mess of minerals, bacteria and liquid into frogs and ferns and fjords.

In our second passage, from Acts, we are at another new beginning. We see the disciples huddled together in their room, with no shape or pattern to their future lives now that Jesus has left them. The Holy Spirit has been hovering again, though! He bursts into their prayers, turns everything topsy-turvy and takes Jesus' followers off in new and wonderful directions.

God has gone before us, preparing the way before we even dream of joining in with him. I love to imagine those huge, soft, feathery wings wrapped around myself, my family and friends, the Holy Spirit brooding over our lives, and, when the time is right, filling us with his vision and energy to move forward into what he has prepared for us.

Prayer

Lord, thank you for hovering over the mess and muddle of our lives. Fill us with your Holy Spirit so that we can keep on joining in your wonderful work of creation and recreation in the world.

Genesis 2:4–9 (NIV)

Messy Creator

This is the account of the heavens and the earth when they were created. When the Lord God made the earth and the heavens—and no shrub of the field had yet appeared on the earth and no plant of the field had yet sprung up, for the Lord God had not sent rain on the earth and there was no man to work the ground, but streams came up from the earth and watered the whole surface of the ground—the Lord God formed the man from the dust of the ground and breathed into his nostrils the breath of life, and the man became a living being. Now the Lord God had planted a garden in the east, in Eden; and there he put the man he had formed. And the Lord God made all kinds of trees grow out of the ground—trees that were pleasing to the eye and good for food.

God got his hands dirty! What a very earthy passage this is: we can picture God with his hands in a pile of mud, squeezing and stroking a human form out of it—very messy, as anyone who has tried their hand at sculpting with clay will appreciate. He seems childlike, keen to experience the world through touch. Not content with being a sculptor, he is also shown as a gardener, planting a garden in Eden. Is it possible to garden without getting dirty? No. God got stuck in, heedless of the cost to his dignity.

God's palmprints are all over the earth he made. His love for the planet and everyone and everything on it is not a distant, aloof love, but an intimate, physical love. He gets involved with his creation, knows what grit, sand and water feel like, knows the warmth of a hand's touch on skin. As we follow in his footsteps, do we get involved with our planet or do we stay aloof from it? Do we get involved with the people around us or do we stay at a safe distance? Are we ready to get our hands dirty in loving service of our communities?

Prayer

Creator God, help us reflect who you are to those we meet today.

Genesis 11:4–8 (NIV, abridged)

Messed-up world

Then they said, 'Come, let us build ourselves a city, with a tower that reaches to the heavens, so that we may make a name for ourselves and not be scattered over the face of the whole earth.'… The Lord said, '… Come, let us go down and confuse their language so they will not understand each other.' So the Lord scattered them from there over all the earth, and they stopped building the city.

Here we see a dangerous tidiness and a painful messiness. How tidy, efficient and productive these people in the Babylonian plain were! Like a production line in a burger chain, the people start to make amazing progress with the city and tower, but their aims are fundamentally flawed. Their organised arrogance causes their downfall: their selfish ambition and efficiency build God completely out of the project. In their conveyor belt success, there was no space for the Spirit to move.

The mess that ensues is not the creative mess of the Creator God, but a chaotic confusion, bringing destruction and separation that are only healed centuries later when the Holy Spirit turns the babble of foreign languages into speech everyone can understand at Pentecost (Acts 2:6–8).

Keeping the balance between sensible, responsible planning and sensitive responsiveness to God is not easy. We need to listen to the Spirit who broods in us, weaves in and out of scripture and breathes through the lives and words of people around us as we live fully in the present and plan wisely for the future. Rapid growth may be, but is not necessarily, godly, whether it is in an organisation, a church or a person. Jesus' images of the kingdom of heaven included seeds and yeast, both of which need space and time to mature. Imagine if the Babylonians had sought God's blessing for their building projects and dedicated them to his glory, building them in his way. Maybe then (to rephrase verse 6 from the Genesis passage), 'nothing they planned to do would have been impossible for them'.

Prayer

Lord, open my eyes to the areas of my life where I am only empire-building and help me instead to grow the kingdom.

Exodus 31:1–6 (NIV, abridged)

Getting messy

Then the Lord said to Moses, 'See, I have chosen Bezalel… and I have filled him with the Spirit of God, with skill, ability and knowledge in all kinds of crafts—to make artistic designs for work in gold, silver and bronze, to cut and set stones, to work in wood, and to engage in all kinds of craftsmanship… Also I have given skill to all the craftworkers to make everything I have commanded you.'

There was an important job to be done: a tabernacle had to be provided, a visible dwelling place for God among his people. This was not a job for the great speakers or holy priests, the wise scribes or the learned historians: this vital job called for people who were good with their hands. Bezalel was 'filled with the Spirit of God'—that is, his creative skills were inspired and blessed by God. Can you imagine Bezalel gleefully sketching out designs that poured directly from the Holy Spirit living in him?

In the passage we see the respect that God has for people who work with their hands and the joy he takes in their hard-earned 'skill, ability and knowledge'—all three aspects of craftsmanship working together for the glory of God.

At Messy Churches we often find that the adults who come along are reluctant to get their hands dirty or risk making or drawing things, although the children rarely have such qualms. This is symptomatic of the lack of respect in our country for practical skills. Perhaps, too, it says something about learning from children about how to become more fully the people we were made to be—imaginative, creative, spontaneous, adaptive, responsive. As we let go of our unwillingness to take risks and fears about what other people will think of us, we can be more open to following the promptings of the Spirit within us. This openness may not result in lampstands and woven garments, but may lead us to a dimension of life that we have never dared venture into.

Reflection

What does it mean to you that Jesus worked with his hands?

Thursday

Genesis 50:19–21 (NIV)

Messy families

> But Joseph said to [his brothers], 'Don't be afraid. Am I in the place of
> God? You intended to harm me, but God intended it for good to accom-
> plish what is now being done, the saving of many lives. So then, don't
> be afraid. I will provide for you and your children.' And he reassured
> them and spoke kindly to them.

My favourite book when I was pregnant was *How Not to be a Perfect Mother*
by Libby Purves. Instead of setting out unrealisable ideals, it gave me a
picture of real, fallible women doing their best to cope with real children.
My own firstborn did not keep to the rules of child development and, until
he was given the diagnosis of Asperger's syndrome (an autistic spectrum
disorder), made us feel that we were useless parents. A friend with a child
who also has Asperger's tearfully described the hostile reaction that she
and her child received at their church when he behaved 'inappropriately'
(and she is the minister's wife!).

Do churches expect families to be perfect before they can come in?
Do we communicate the message that church is only for the neat families whose children are immaculately behaved and whose parenting skills
are honed to perfection? What open and subliminal messages does your
church give to families, be they regular members or occasional visitors, who
are, quite frankly, a mess—where the adults' behaviour is 'appalling', the
children are 'naughty' and the teenagers 'impossible'?

An unsuccessful search for a perfect Old Testament family has made me
realise that God, as well as Libby Purves, has a very realistic view of family
life: the families depicted in the various books are messy. Perhaps God's
redemption comes through mess rather than tidiness.

The esteemed patriarch Jacob was head of a family renowned for its dys-
functional nature. Even after their father's death, Joseph's brothers are still
lying and cheating to save their own necks (vv. 15–17). Joseph, nobody's
fool, and certainly no paragon himself, can see beyond the mess to the bigger picture of God's redemptive plan. Do we share this vision of hope with
the messy families we know?

Prayer

Lord, show me the good in the families I meet today.

Luke 2:4–7 (NIV, abridged)

Messy incarnation

So Joseph... went [to Bethlehem] to register with Mary, who was pledged to be married to him and was expecting a child. While they were there, the time came for the baby to be born, and she gave birth to her firstborn, a son. She wrapped him in cloths and placed him in a manger, because there was no room for them in the inn.

How would you come to earth if you were God? I think I would opt for an entrance like the Greek goddess Athena—leaping out of a skull in a full suit of armour has definite style! Another option would be being brought up safely in the confines of a remote palace, as was Prince Siddhartha Gautama (later known as Buddha). I would not choose to be born as a baby into circumstances that combine dubious parentage, shattered reputations, political oppression, less than luxurious circumstances and imminent danger of genocide. This would not be romantic, heroic or comfy.

If we remove the tidy images of Christmas (when did you last see a cow pat on a Christmas card?), what does it say to us, this messy start in life that Jesus chose for himself? Perhaps it is another aspect of the view God takes of family life that we began to think about yesterday. If Jesus himself chose to be born into a family, could this mean that God sees the messy nature of a family environment as the best possible way to become a fully human person? Also, would this imply a call to Jesus' church to be a family to its members, young and old, single and married, to help them all become as fully human as they could, from birth through to death?

Mary knew that the birth of Jesus would not only turn her own ordered family life into an unpredictable adventure but it would also overturn the world order itself, with the big cheeses being replaced with small fry, hungry people feasting and rich people left unsatisfied. Her song in Luke 1 is not one of fear, however, but of glory in God's unruliness.

Prayer

Pray for your church family to be 'simply one more device for dragging in Love'
(C.S. Lewis, The Screwtape Letters, 1942).

Matthew 9:10–13 (NIV)

----- Jesus and tidy people -----

While Jesus was having dinner at Matthew's house, many tax collectors and 'sinners' came and ate with him and his disciples. When the Pharisees saw this, they asked his disciples, 'Why does your teacher eat with tax collectors and "sinners"?' On hearing this, Jesus said, 'It is not the healthy who need a doctor, but the sick. But go and learn what this means: "I desire mercy, not sacrifice." For I have not come to call the righteous, but sinners.'

If I had been around during Jesus' ministry, I would probably have been cheering on the Pharisees. They were so holy! They get a bad press in the Gospels, but they were the great religious role models of their day, super-spiritual, steeped in prayer and with vast reservoirs of wisdom to draw on. They studied the scriptures to a degree that most of us cannot imagine and many had a deep desire to serve God 'properly'. I can only hope that the questions they hurled at Jesus and his disciples came from a sincere wish to do the right thing in God's eyes, rather than out of a desire to trip Jesus up. Here he was, this amateur from the back of beyond, eating with outsiders, untouchables, giving a view of God and the faith that might bring the whole structure tumbling down, unless the guardians remained vigilant. Of course he should be challenged!

Jesus has a bigger view than just keeping to the rules, however. He sees not only the letter but the spirit of the law, because he himself is not only the *logos*, the Word of the Law, but also the Spirit of the Law. He deliberately seeks out people whose lives are in such a mess that the name 'sinners' has to suffice to describe their depravity. You can imagine Jesus looking up from his eating couch beside an unrepentant tax collector, a sniggering working girl perched by his feet with a wine jug, to see those disapproving faces looking down on him. Even so, he does not humiliate them. 'Go and learn,' he urges them, seeing the limits of their understanding but in complete confidence that God's love encompasses them as well as the 'sinners'.

Prayer

Lord, help us to go and learn the unregulated boundlessness of your love.

Matthew 20:30–34 (NIV)

‑‑‑‑‑ Jesus and messy people ‑‑‑‑‑

Two blind men were sitting by the roadside, and when they heard that Jesus was going by, they shouted, 'Lord, Son of David, have mercy on us!' The crowd rebuked them and told them to be quiet, but they shouted all the louder, 'Lord, Son of David, have mercy on us!' Jesus stopped and called them. 'What do you want me to do for you?' he asked. 'Lord,' they answered, 'we want our sight.' Jesus had compassion on them and touched their eyes. Immediately they received their sight and followed him.

Not everyone knows how to behave. GPs complain about patients taking mobile phone calls while they are in the middle of intimate medical procedures. Theatre audiences become irate at school groups texting during a performance. Not removing baseball caps in any remotely formal setting is also a source of irritation.

There is a kind of messy behaviour that is simply antisocial, putting self above the good of others, and needs to be transformed so that all can enjoy life to the full. Another kind of messy behaviour, exhibited by the men in this passage, breaks the rules, offends and shocks, but is appropriate because it is governed by godly priorities. The men wanted Jesus to heal them and no one was going to get in their way.

We have been good at rebuking people in church. In our work with BRF's Barnabas ministries, for instance, we hear countless stories from people who have been rebuked for the way their children behave in church. When the crowd prevented them from coming to Jesus, these two men simply shouted all the louder. For many people, though, who have less confidence or faith than these men, whose lives are in a messy patch, when faced with rebuke it is easier to fall silent, back away and melt out of the church door, taking their unmet needs with them.

These messy men hollered until Jesus heard them. He had compassion, came close and met their need. I wonder what form the 'hollering' of people around us takes when they long to be close to Jesus.

Prayer

Lord Jesus, help us to hear the needs behind the messy behaviour in our communities and to help people come close to you.

Luke 22:17–20 (NIV)

Jesus' messy meals

After taking the cup, [Jesus] gave thanks and said, 'Take this and divide it among you. For I tell you I will not drink again of the fruit of the vine until the kingdom of God comes.' And he took bread, gave thanks and broke it, and gave it to them, saying, 'This is my body given for you; do this in remembrance of me.' In the same way, after the supper he took the cup, saying, 'This cup is the new covenant in my blood, which is poured out for you.'

If you think of it purely from an objective point of view, eating is a pretty revolting process. Lumps of nutrients are forked into an orifice, the jaws chomp it all into a mush, saliva and gastric juices flow. It is amazing how sharing this messy act has bonded human communities together, over millennia. Logically, it should be done in isolation, as a matter of necessity, rather than as the gloriously public celebration of intimacy that it is. Meals may be messy, bodily and basic, but to human beings they are also miraculous, symbolic and multidimensional.

Jesus ate with anyone who would have him at a time when it was even more significant to break bread with someone than it is now. To do so was to identify with them and accept their way of life, giving them a glimpse of the heavenly banquet—and Jesus banqueted with the wrong people! No wonder he got into trouble. No wonder eyes narrowed when the 'sinful' woman poured her perfume over Jesus during a meal. No wonder Martha, Zacchaeus and Levi changed so profoundly and swiftly after sharing food with Jesus. Through his acceptance of hospitality from anyone who would offer it, Jesus showed his love, welcome and joy in them. He was the perfect guest.

How did he invite us to mark his death and resurrection? With the invitation to take, eat, drink. The ordinary intimacy of a shared meal becomes an extraordinary intimacy with the past story and future glory, a moment of timelessness in that most earthly mouthful—a chunk of bread, a sip of wine, open to everyone. He was and is the perfect host.

Prayer

Lord, help us to invite all those messy people—like the ones who invited you to their tables—to come to yours.

Dyffryn Ardudwy in the Welsh Diocese of Bangor is the 500th Messy Church

July 2010 was a major month in the life of the Dyffryn Ardudwy church. It was the month when all things Messy oozed and splashed its way in multi colours out into this small community in Gwynedd, North Wales.

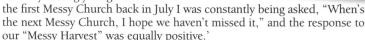

The Rector, Revd Stephanie Beacon, reflects, 'Messy Church has breathed new life and energy into our parish's ministry among young families. After the first Messy Church back in July I was constantly being asked, "When's the next Messy Church, I hope we haven't missed it," and the response to our "Messy Harvest" was equally positive.'

Another leader, Beth Bailey, who is the Diocesan Children's Work Adviser in Bangor, says, 'We gave out feedback forms at our first Messy Church: To the question 'Did you enjoy it?', all the answers were positive ranging from 'Yes' to many 'fantastics' and 'brilliants'. The only response to 'What would you change?' was 'We need a bigger hall!,' which was true because for many it was standing room only! '

'This is the second Messy Church running in Bangor Diocese. Both are very popular and for me the extraordinary response has been both humbling and challenging,' concludes Beth. Dyffryn's Messy Church is held on a Monday and always includes a welcome drink as the families arrives, a wide range of crafts and messy play, a time of worship with lively songs and a simple meal so the youngest leave tired, happy and ready for bed.

Luke 23:44–47 (NIV)

Messy death

> It was now about the sixth hour, and darkness came over the whole land until the ninth hour, for the sun stopped shining. And the curtain of the temple was torn in two. Jesus called out with a loud voice, 'Father, into your hands I commit my spirit.' When he had said this, he breathed his last. The centurion, seeing what had happened, praised God and said, 'Surely this was a righteous man.'

This was not noble or heroic or uplifting. It was not wondrous, glorious or triumphant, not at the time. It was embarrassing, degrading, confused, a mistake, a mess.

At a production of *Coriolanus*, I watched an actress showing a moment of profound grief—her beautiful face became distorted, her features grotesque, unrecognisable. She was no longer a glamorous figure but one you would back away from. She showed something of that picture of the Suffering Servant in Isaiah 53:3: 'Like one from whom men hide their faces.' I close my eyes at gruesome bits in films. I turn away.

The Gospel writers did not need to spell out the horrific nature of crucifixion as their readers would have seen the devastation it wrought on a human body. We can only imagine. It might be tempting to tidy up Jesus' death into a neat crucifix on a pretty chain, to remember only the resurrection and make no imaginative attempt to see his familiar body, one that we have sat with and laughed with and eaten with and walked with, pathetically exposed and open to the cruelty of the mob.

It is only when we accept this ravaged destruction of Jesus, however, that we can begin to glimpse the depth of God's commitment to us. It is only when we accept his broken, gutted, ridiculous humiliation that we guess at the unlimited understanding he has of any suffering we might be going through in our own lives. It is only through this hideous mess that the miracle of redemption can take place. We would all rather it happened in another way, without the pain or the humiliation for our gentle friend. The crucifixion, though, more than any other choice Jesus made in his life, shows that mess is where God can work miracles.

Prayer

My God, what love is this?

Luke 24:9–12 (NIV)

- - - - - - Messy resurrection - - - - - -

When [the women] came back from the tomb, they told all these things to the Eleven and to all the others... But they did not believe the women, because their words seemed to them like nonsense. Peter, however, got up and ran to the tomb. Bending over, he saw the strips of linen lying by themselves, and he went away, wondering to himself what had happened.

We do a lot of storytelling in our work with Barnabas and are continually amazed at the way story works so powerfully in people's lives. Only the other day a colleague was describing the imaginative response a group of children made to the story of Mary, mother of Jesus. When we're preparing stories, it's always a challenge as to how to present the sequence of events, what to highlight, what to filter out. The Gospel writers seem to face the same problem with the resurrection! In what order did it all happen? What's most important when you have angels and earthquakes and rolled stones and linen cloths and women, all clamouring to be mentioned? We wouldn't call the resurrection accounts a mess, but neither would anybody call it a tidy and logical story. Things were happening that went beyond rational cataloguing and we are presented with a range of different viewpoints and impressions, like many different TV channels at a great international event, rather than a neat happy ending.

The Gospel writers knew better than to offer a fairytale ending—'and they all lived happily ever after'. The wondering, disbelief, puzzlement, lack of faith, lack of understanding, squabbling and discontent continued even after the disciples had all met Jesus personally in his post-resurrection body: God knows we don't come to the end of our journey this side of death: new possibilities open up during the whole of our lives. The artist Matisse designed a chapel in Vence in France where the stained glass tree of life shouts of resurrection hope: he was in his 80s when he did the work for this glorious place. He was still discovering, still exploring, still creating right to the end of his life.

Prayer

Lord of life, help us to see our unfinished stories as a blessing.

1 Corinthians 12:21–24 (NIV)

Messy church

The eye cannot say to the hand, 'I don't need you!' And the head cannot say to the feet, 'I don't need you!' On the contrary, those parts of the body that seem to be weaker are indispensable, and the parts that we think are less honourable we treat with special honour. And the parts that are unpresentable are treated with special modesty, while our presentable parts need no special treatment.

There is a temptation to idealise the early Church, despite all the evidence that the churches Paul helped to establish were just as imperfect as the ones we belong to.

Paul wrote, 'We… are being transformed into [Jesus'] likeness' (2 Corinthians 3:18). He did not claim that the believers had been made perfect already and were forming a church of utopian perfection, but, rather, every human being is a work in progress. While characters and relationships are being transformed, this means that there will be a certain amount of messiness in a Christian community, as we see in the image of the body in the passage above.

For Paul, a body cannot be uniform or it is not a body at all. A body needs different parts with wildly different functions and shapes. It may look less tidy and be less 'efficient' than a machine, but the body of Christ, the Church—with all of us messy 'works in progress' as its different limbs and organs—is the way God has chosen to carry on Jesus' redeeming work in the world. He delights in this messiness.

I have another work in progress of my own—a roll of lining paper that travels round with me on my BRF travels. At each Messy Church event, I invite people to draw on it the part of the anatomy of the body of Christ they think they are. The more that are added from Ireland, Bedford, London, Cwmbran or Dorchester, the more I see the 'ever-increasing glory' Paul writes about.

Are there any people to whom your church is effectively saying, 'We don't need you'?

Prayer

Lord, help us recognise the 'unpresentable' parts in our churches. Show us how to honour them.

Galatians 5:22–26 (NIV)

Messy discipleship

But the fruit of the Spirit is love, joy, peace, patience, kindness, good-ness, faithfulness, gentleness and self-control. Against such things there is no law. Those who belong to Christ Jesus have crucified the sinful nature with its passions and desires. Since we live by the Spirit, let us keep in step with the Spirit. Let us not become conceited, pro-voking and envying each other.

Wouldn't it be easy if we had a chart to tick off whether we were being a good disciple or not? '24 June: Oh, yes, I did patience this morning at 10.34, tick that. Can't tick off peace today, so I'll have to do two lots of kindness tomorrow to get up to speed again…' It would be so tidy, so easy to see if we were holy or not.

Paul does not give us rules and regulations, though. Instead, he shows us that Jesus' followers are living from the inside out—with the Spirit on the inside, working with us, cheering us on, holding us back, daring us to risk more, comforting us, always nudging us closer to Jesus. How could you systemise this sort of progress? Discipleship is not a set of achievements but a relationship, a way of life. Any help with discipleship needs to be like a tour guide showing you parts of a city that you would never have reached without them, not a route marked out with no possibility of deviation.

How do we react to people whose discipleship path turns out very dif-ferent from our own? How quick are we to label them 'liberal', 'extremist', 'happy clappy'? How much do we delight in seeing God's Spirit alive and working in them, even if it is in a completely different way from how he works in us?

Think of the people you have responsibility for. How can you encourage them today into greater love, moments of joy, peace that the world cannot give, a patience that never gives up, goodness providing a light in a dark world, faithfulness hanging on like a limpet, gentleness that gives others space or self-control that puts others first every time?

Prayer

Lord, help me to listen to your Spirit today.

Luke 15:22–24 (NIV)

Messy celebration

> But the father said to his servants, 'Quick! Bring the best robe and put it on him. Put a ring on his finger and sandals on his feet. Bring the fattened calf and kill it. Let's have a feast and celebrate. For this son of mine was dead and is alive again; he was lost and is found.' So they began to celebrate.

The journey is over. The traveller has come home and found a rapturous welcome, way beyond what he was expecting. Surely this is a picture of the homecoming we ultimately long for—unconditional forgiveness, unreserved joy, the open arms of a father we thought we might never see again and old friends running to rejoice with us that we are back with them in this wonderful place that is both work and home. Relationships have been restored, everything is whole and the only response is to party—and what a party it is!

Sometimes this parable is told as if it finished there, but, of course, the crucial punchline is how the older son reacts and how the father reacts to him, and yet we do not know how it ends! Even in this picture of what heaven itself may be like, it is messy. The apparently good, hardworking, devoted son has shut himself out and the layabout younger brother is right there at the centre of the celebration. It is not fair! There are people at the party who do not deserve to be there.

The parables about the heavenly feast (Luke 14:16–24; Matthew 22:1–14) do not show the rigid righteousness and earned rewards that the Pharisees seemed to want. As in his actual meals with society's outcasts, Jesus showed them a heaven full of scruffs from the highways and byways who were hauled in at the last minute. On the cross, he promised paradise to a thief who certainly had not had time to do a confirmation course. By the illimitable grace of God, the kingdom of heaven is open to those people we are quite certain will not be there. By the illimitable grace of God, even we can be there.

Prayer

Lord, thank you that we might be sitting at your banquet next to any one of the people we encounter today.

Parenting Children for a Life of Faith

Helping children meet and know God

Rachel Turner

Parenting Children for a Life of Faith explores how the home can become the primary place in which children are nurtured into the reality of God's presence and love, equipped to access him themselves and encouraged to grow in a two-way relationship with him that will last a lifetime.

The basic idea behind the ideas explored is that we need to model for our children what it means to be in a relationship with God rather than just equipping them to know about him—helping our children to be God-connected rather than just God-smart.

The material is organised into three parts, which look at:

- Discipling our children proactively
- Modelling the reality of being in a relationship with God
- Tying together truth and experience
- Connecting children to God's heart
- Implementing a plan

Each chapter includes encouraging true stories and questions to help you reflect on your own experience as we journey together with our children.

978 1 84101 607 8, pb, £7.99

Messy Church is growing!

Every month families who have never set foot in a church before are enjoying Messy Church. And every month more Messy Churches are started all over the UK and worldwide, sharing God's good news with families across denominations and church traditions.

Messy Church is enabled, resourced and supported by BRF (Bible Reading Fellowship), a Registered Charity, as one of its core ministries. BRF makes Messy Church freely available and derives no direct income from the work that we do to support it both in the UK and abroad.

Would you be willing to support this ministry with your prayer and your giving? To find out more visit **www.messychurch.org.uk/champions**

Messy Church
Fresh ideas for building a Christ-centred community
Lucy Moore

Overflowing with creative ideas to draw the community together for fun, food, fellowship and worship, this resource book contains 15 themed programme outlines. Each outline has ideas for creative art and craft activities, meal plans and recipes for eating together and family-friendly worship.

978 1 84101 503 3, pb, £8.99

Messy Church 2
Ideas for discipling a Christ-centred community
Lucy Moore

Contains a further 15 units of fun, food, crafts and mess, with a year's worth of material that your Messy Church will love. The material also includes many ideas for practical ways to promote a sense of fellowship and community.

978 1 84101 602 3, pb, £8.99

Messy Crafts
A craft-based journal for Messy Church members
Lucy Moore

Messy Crafts has plenty of categorised craft ideas to help plan a Messy Church but can also be used as a scrapbook or notebook at home, with prayers to draw and colour and stick as well as things to make.

978 1 84101 816 4, pb, £6.99

Messy Cooks
A handbook for Messy Church catering teams
Jane Butcher

Messy Cooks is a handbook for cooks' teams, which can also be used in the home as a source of good recipes.

978 1 84101 814 0, pb, £5.99

New Daylight
Your daily Bible reading, comment and prayer
Edited by Naomi Starkey

New Daylight offers four months of daily Bible reading and reflection, published January, May and September. An ideal way to start reading from the Bible every day. It contains daily Bible readings (with Bible text included), comments from the contributor and a prayer or reflection. It also notes some of the special festivals that make up the Church calendar, to help readers appreciate the riches of the Christian year.

Contributors include Helen Julian CSF, Margaret Silf, John Proctor, David Winter and many more, each bringing their own unique interpretation to different stories or characters of the Bible.

New Daylight is available in **standard pocket size** format, a **deluxe edition** (desk diary size with higher-quality paper and larger font size), **by email** delivered straight to your inbox every morning and as an **app for your iPhone**, iPad or iPod touch. For more details about the app, to see sample pages and to get your **free trial** of the app, visit **www.biblereadingnotes. org.uk/iphone-apps/**

See the subscription order form on page 22 for prices.

Day by Day with God
Rooting women's lives in the Bible
Edited by Catherine Butcher

Treat yourself to time out with God every day! Published every four months in January, May and September, *Day by Day with God* provides a short printed Bible passage, explained and applied especially for women, by women. A suggested daily prayer or meditation, plus further reading to explore which help readers connect the Bible passage with their own lives, and with their spiritual journeys as they seek to follow Jesus more closely.

Contributors to *Day by Day with God* include Wendy Bray, Wendy Virgo, Jean Watson, Alie Stibbe and many more. For more details and to see sample pages, visit **www.biblereadingnotes.org.uk**.

See the subscription order form on page 22 for prices.

ORDER FORM

New Daylight and *Day by Day with God* one year subscriptions

- Three editions of *New Daylight* or *Day by Day with God*
- Includes postage and packing
- Each edition has four months of readings
- *New Daylight* and *Day by Day with God* are published January, May and September

Subscription order form

Quantity Required	Product Code	Title	Price UK only	Total Cost
	One-Year Subscription	Day by Day with God—I wish to start my subscription in Jan, May, Sep (circle month required)	£15.15	
	One-Year Subscription	New Daylight—I wish to start my subscription in Jan, May, Sep (circle month required)	£14.70	
		Subscription order value		

Book order form

Quantity Required	Product Code	Title	Price	Total Cost
	978 1 84101 503 3	Messy Church	£8.99	
	978 1 84101 602 3	Messy Church 2	£8.99	
	978 1 84101 849 2	Messy Church the DVD	£9.99	
	978 1 84101 814 0	Messy Cooks	£5.99	
	978 1 84101 816 4	Messy Crafts	£6.99	
	978 0 85746 008 0	Messy Readings	£1.00	
	978 1 84101 607 8	Parenting Children for a Life of Faith	£7.99	

Postage and packing charges				
order value	UK	Total book order		
£7.00 & under	£1.25	Add postage and packing (see opposite)		
£7.01–£30.00	£2.25	Book order value		
Over £30.00	free	Subscription order value		
		Total order value		

Customers ordering from outside the UK should refer to www.brfonline.org.uk for subscription, post and packing charges.

Prices on all titles may change at the discretion of BRF.